Stories
of
GREAT PEOPLE

Galileo's telescope

Gerry Bailey and Karen Foster
Illustrated by Leighton Noyes
and Karen Radford

🌳 Crabtree Publishing Company
www.crabtreebooks.com

HANNAH PLATT is Digby's argumentative, older sister—and she doesn't believe a word that Mr. Rummage says!

DIGBY PLATT is an antique collector. Every Saturday he picks up a bargain at Mr. Rummage's antique stall and loves listening to the story behind his new 'find'.

Mr. RUMMAGE has a stall piled high with interesting objects—and he has a great story to tell about each and every one of his treasures.

Crabtree Publishing Company
www.crabtreebooks.com

Other books in the series
Armstrong's moon rock
Cleopatra's coin
Columbus's chart
Julius Caesar's sandals
Leonardo's palette
Queen Victoria's diamond
Marco Polo's silk purse
Martin Luther King Jr.'s microphone
Mother Teresa's alms bowl
Mozart's wig
Queen Victoria's diamond
Shakespeare's quill
Sitting Bull's tomahawk
The Wright Brothers' glider

Credits
The Art Archive: Civiche Racc. d'Arte Pavia Italy/Dagli Orti:
    p. 32 (top right); Musée Granet Aix-en-Provence/Dagli Orti:
    p. 30 (bottom left); Observatory Academy Florence Italy /Dagli Orti:
    p. 11 (right), 27 (top right); Palazzo Chigi Siena/Dagli Orti:
    p. 29 (center left); Private Collection Paris /Dagli Orti:
    p. 15 (bottom left); Querini Stampalia Foundation Venice/Dagli Orti:
    p. 17 (bottom left); National Gallery London / Eileen Tweedy:
    p. 15 (top right); Private Collection/Eileen Tweedy: p. 30 (top right)
Private Collection/©Christie's Images/Bridgeman Art Library: p. 25 (right)
Mary Evans Picture Library: 17 (top right), 20 (top right), 27 (bottom left)
Topfoto: Fotomas: p. 29 (top right); HIP: p. 13 (bottom left),
    19 (bottom); Roger-Viollet: p. 13 (top right); Charles Walker:
    p. 10 (bottom), 18 (bottom right), 19 (top), 20 (bottom left),
    21 (bottom)
Rijksmuseum, Amsterdam: p. 23 (bottom)
R. Sheridan/Ancient Art & Architecture Collection: p. 9

Picture research: Diana Morris. info@picture-research.co.uk
Editor: Lynn Peppas
Proofreaders: David Hurd, Crystal Sikkens
Project editor: Robert Walker
Prepress technician: Ken Wright
Production coordinator: Margaret Amy Salter

Library and Archives Canada Cataloguing in Publication

Bailey, Gerry
   Galileo's telescope / Gerry Bailey and Karen Foster ; illustrated
by Leighton Noyes and Karen Radford.

(Stories of great people)
Includes index.
ISBN 978-0-7787-3694-3 (bound).--ISBN 978-0-7787-3716-2 (pbk.)

   1. Galilei, Galileo, 1564-1642--Juvenile fiction. 2. Astronomers--Italy--
Biography--Juvenile fiction. 3. Mathematicians--Italy--Biography--Juvenile fiction.
4. Scientists--Italy--Biography--Juvenile fiction. 5. Galilei, Galileo, 1564-1642--
Juvenile literature. 6. Astronomers--Italy--Biography--Juvenile literature.
7. Mathematicians--Italy--Biography--Juvenile literature. 8. Scientists--Italy--
Biography--Juvenile literature. I. Noyes, Leighton II. Radford, Karen III. Foster,
Karen, 1959- IV. Title. V. Series.

PZ7.B15Ga 2008   j823'.92   C2008-907335-5

Library of Congress Cataloging-in-Publication Data

Bailey, Gerry.
  Galileo's telescope / Gerry Bailey and Karen Foster ; illustrated by
Leighton Noyes and Karen Radford.
    p. cm. -- (Stories of great people)
  Includes index.
  ISBN 978-0-7787-3716-2 (pbk. : alk. paper) -- ISBN 978-0-7787-3694-3
(reinforced lib. bdg. : alk. paper)
  1. Galilei, Galileo, 1564-1642. 2.
Astronomers--Italy--Biography--Juvenile literature. 3.
Mathematicians--Italy--Biography--Juvenile literature. 4.
Scientists--Italy--Biography--Juvenile literature. I. Foster, Karen,
1959- II. Noyes, Leighton, ill. III. Radford, Karen, ill. IV. Title.

  QB36.G2B27 2009
  520.92--dc22
  [B]
                     2008048636

Crabtree Publishing Company
www.crabtreebooks.com   1-800-387-7650

Published in Canada
Crabtree Publishing
616 Welland Ave.
St. Catharines, Ontario
L2M 5V6

Published in the United States
Crabtree Publishing
PMB16A
350 Fifth Ave., Suite 3308
New York, NY 10118

Published by CRABTREE PUBLISHING COMPANY
Copyright © 2009 Diverta Ltd.

Galileo's telescope
Table of Contents

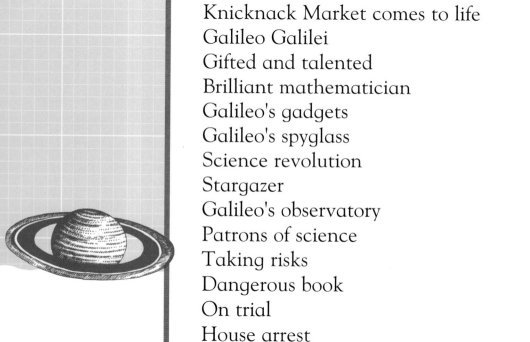
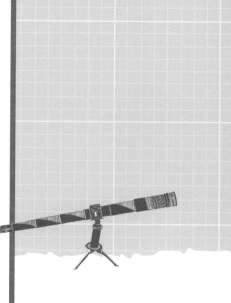

Every Saturday morning, Knicknack Market comes to life. The street vendors are there almost before the Sun is up. And by the time you and I have got out of bed, the stalls are built, the boxes opened, and all the goods carefully laid out on display.

Objects are piled high. Some are laid out on velvet: precious necklaces and jeweled swords. Others stand upright at the back:

large, framed pictures of very important people, lamps made from tasseled satin, and old-fashioned cash registers—the kind that jingle when the drawers are opened. And then there are things that stay in their boxes all day, waiting for the right customer to come along: war medals laid out in straight lines, stopwatches on leather straps, and cutlery in polished silver for all those special occasions.

But Mr. Rummage's stall is different. Mr. Rummage of Knicknack Market has a stall piled high with a disorderly jumble of things that no one could ever want. Who'd want to buy a stuffed mouse? Or a broken umbrella? Or a pair of false teeth?

Mr. Rummage has them all, and, as you can imagine, they don't cost a lot!

Rummage's "Antiques"

Digby Platt—ten-year-old collector of antiques—was off to see his friend Mr. Rummage of Knicknack Market. It was Saturday and, as usual, Digby's weekly allowance was burning a hole in his pocket.

Digby wasn't going to spend it on any old thing. It had to be something rare and interesting for his collection, something from Mr. Rummage's incredible stall. Hannah, his older sister, had come along too. She had secret doubts about the value of Mr. Rummage's objects and felt, for some big-sisterly reason, that she had to stop her little brother from buying useless bits of junk.

"Hi, Mr Rummage," said Hannah, feeling bright and cheery for once—and not her usual grumpy self. "Hey, that looks really neat—it's a telescope, right?"

Digby, who wasn't used to his sister taking an interest in anything on Mr. Rummage's stall until she knew a bit more about it, said, "of course it's a telescope, silly, what else could it be?"

"Something to knock you on the head with, perhaps?" said Hannah, grimly.

"Hello you two. Nice to see you've brought a bit of peace and quiet to Knicknack Market." grinned Mr. Rummage. "And, yes, it is a telescope."

"It looks really old," said Hannah, picking it up and examining it.

"That's because it was made almost 500 years ago by the great scientist and astronomer Galileo Galilei."

Hannah beamed, "That's fab—I'm really into all that stars and planets stuff."

 # Galileo Galilei

Galileo Galilei was born on February 15, 1564, in Pisa, Italy. He was one of seven children, the first child of Vincenzo Galilei and Giulia degli Ammannati. His parents were noble but poor.

Galileo was a **mathematician, physicist,** and **astronomer** whose discoveries challenged scientific ideas that had been accepted for thousands of years. Using his telescope, he changed people's view of the solar system and the way the Sun, Moon, stars, and planets like Earth, moved within it.

But let's find out more...

"No wonder they didn't have much money—with all those kids," said Hannah. "So where did Galileo live?"

"He was born in an Italian town called Pisa," said Mr. Rummage.

"That's where the famous leaning tower is, isn't it?" said Hannah.

"That's right. Galileo was brought up in the Catholic faith and sent to a monastery school at the age of 11," said Mr. Rummage. "So he knew the Bible off by heart, I bet," said Digby.

"I expect he knew it pretty well," replied Mr. Rummage, "but he was also keen on math and geometry, and would have studied the ideas of many scientists."

"Is that when he decided to become an astronomer, then?" asked Hannah.

"You'd think so, but at the age of 14 he wanted to become a monk. He liked the religious life, you see," said Mr. Rummage. "But his father wanted him to be a merchant so he could earn a decent living. Galileo refused, though, point blank. He was already showing signs of being a bit of a rebel."

Gifted and talented

Galileo's father was a cloth merchant by trade, but he was also a very artistic man—a musician, a composer, and a mathematician. Galileo grew up to love music too, and from a very early age played the lute, a kind of guitar. In time, he became a brilliant lutist. He also painted and sketched well. Some people believe he really wanted to be a painter, and not a scientist at all. But his natural talent for mathematics probably made the difference.

Student doctor

When Galileo showed no signs of following in his father's footsteps, Vincenzo decided his son should become a doctor. This time, Galileo was forced to go along with his father's wishes, and was packed off to the university in Pisa when he was 17.

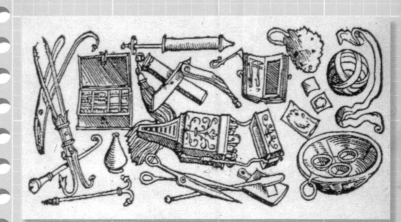

Drop out

Money soon became a problem for young Galileo, and he failed to win a scholarship that would have helped. This may have been because his troublemaking had earned him so many enemies. In the end, he dropped out of the math, and science courses without a degree.

The wrangler

Galileo soon got bored with medicine. He wanted to study math, and played truant so he could do just that. Unfortunately he had a rather disagreeable personality and annoyed his fellow pupils. He was also unpopular with his teachers. In fact, he was nicknamed "the Wrangler" because he loved asking awkward questions and always argued against anything that could not be backed up with solid proof. Some of his teachers probably could not admit the fact that they had spent a lifetime teaching the wrong thing!

Swinging pendulum

In 1581, according to legend, a swinging lamp in Pisa Cathedral caught Galileo's eye. He used his pulse to time the swinging of the lamp and realized that the swings from left to right were even and took exactly the same length of time. Eventually his law of the pendulum led to the development of the pendulum clock. The lamp that hangs there today is named after him, in recognition of his marvellous achievements.

"Poor Galileo," said Hannah, "no money and too much attitude! So how did he get to be a brilliant astronomer?"

"He financed his studies by giving private math lessons to wealthy pupils," replied Mr. Rummage.

"Wish he was around now," said Digby. "I could do with a bit of help myself. My brain's not as big as Galileo's."

"About the size of a walnut, I'd say," said Hannah tartly.

"Galileo was just lucky to be born with the kind of brain that can do math easily," said Mr. Rummage. "Anyway, one of his wealthy pupils was called Guidobaldi del Monte."

"You mean he was bald?" screamed Hannah with delight.

"No, it's an Italian name," laughed Mr. Rummage. "Guidobaldi helped Galileo become a professor of math at Pisa just four years after he'd been thrown out!"

Brilliant mathematician

Galileo began his career by giving a brilliant lecture on hell! He took his inspiration from a long, religious poem called *The Divine Comedy* by the famous Italian poet, Dante. When someone in the audience asked how big hell was—which is a bit like asking how big the sky is —he approached the problem scientifically. Quoting a line from the poem that said: "…the giant Nimrod's face was about as long and just as wide as St Peter's dome in Rome." He worked out that the Devil himself was 2,000 arm-lengths long! The audience was impressed.

This huge sextant was used to measure the distance between stars.

The Leaning Tower of Pisa, where Galileo performed his famous experiment on the force of gravity.

Physics tricks

When he was a student, Galileo had learned the ideas of the famous ancient Greek scientist, Aristotle. Aristotle believed that heavy objects fall faster than light ones. Galileo insisted on testing everything for himself to see if Aristotle was actually right. He sent his students to the top of the famous Leaning Tower of Pisa and got them to drop balls of different weights over the side. They all fell at the same speed, proving Aristotle was wrong. However, contradicting Aristotle's ideas was a risky business, and Galileo was not invited back to the university the next year. That did not keep Galileo out of trouble though. The grand Duke of Pisa's son had invented a giant measuring instrument called a **sextant**. Galileo made fun of it and made a powerful enemy of the Duke's son. He had to leave Pisa.

"So Galileo was out of work again," said Hannah.

"Yes, but once again, good old Guidobaldi del Monte came to the rescue," said Mr. Rummage. "He got Galileo a professorship in geometry and astronomy at the University of Padua—an even more important university than Pisa."

"Good old 'Baldi'"said Digby. "I bet Galileo didn't last very long. He was bound to upset someone, wasn't he?"

"You're absolutely right—eventually he upset people in a big way. But more about that later," replied Mr. Rummage. "In the meantime, Galileo's way of teaching math, as if it were the key to all knowledge, soon began to change people's understanding of the subject—although his students probably thought he was playing games, rather than showing them something useful!"

"They must've been wrong, then," said Hannah, "if he changed the way people thought about the world and everything."

"Yes they were," said Mr. Rummage, "but don't forget people had held their beliefs about the universe for a 1,000 years. Telling them they were wrong was not something ordinary people, or religious thinkers in the Church, wanted to hear.

Just imagine, if someone started telling you the Universe was made of string and said they had proof. Would you believe them?"

"No," said Digby "That's just silly."

Mr. Rummage winked at Hannah, "Remember this day if you ever become an astronomer, my dear—string theory is silly."

Galileo's gadgets

Galileo was not just interested in ideas, he was practical too. In fact, he set up a workshop where he could make useful gadgets, like pumps and measuring devices. They made him a small fortune. His most successful inventions were an early thermometer, called a thermoscope, and a kind of early calculator that solved mathematical problems. The calculator was so popular that two jealous scientists accused Galileo of stealing the idea from them. Galileo took them to court and won the case.

An armillary sphere is a skeleton sphere used to measure the position of the stars. In this sphere, Earth is in the center, with the Sun and Moon moving around it—the Greek system of the universe.

The instruments of the age in this picture include a celestial globe and a white sundial.

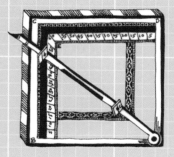

Galileo invented the geometrical and military *proportional* compass, which can be set at any angle.

Money troubles

In 1593, Galileo's father died. This made Galileo head of the family. However, it also made him responsible for his sister's marriage **dowry**—the money a bride's family paid to the groom. A dowry could run to thousands of **crowns**, while Galileo's salary was just 180 crowns. Galileo got badly into debt. Thankfully, his gadgets and the booklets that explained how they worked began selling very well to his rich students, so he just managed to keep out of trouble.

"What about the telescope?" asked Hannah, "did he invent that as well?"

"No," responded Mr. Rummage, "he didn't invent it—he made it more powerful."

"Oh, so this telescope isn't one of his after all," said Digby in a disappointed voice.

"Patience, my dear Digby," said Mr. Rummage. "What you're holding is indeed a masterpiece by the great Galileo, but he called it a spyglass because it was used for spying on…"

"I know—people doing naughty things?" interrupted Digby, mischievously.

"No, no, no… Spyglasses were used to make faraway things look closer."

"Silly boy," said Hannah.

"Hmm," said Mr. Rummage, "Anyway, as soon as Galileo heard that a spyglass had been invented in Holland, he asked for a copy to be sent to him straightaway. When it arrived, he found it could only magnify an object to three times its size," said Mr. Rummage.

"So Galileo decided to make a more powerful one. His first attempt magnified four times. Then it went up to nine, 10 times, and more. Eventually he built one that magnified 30 times."

"Wow!" exclaimed Hannah.

Galileo's spyglass

Galileo made his first "spyglass" in 1609. He modeled it on one made by a Dutch inventor called Lipperhey. The spyglass was made up of a tube with a piece of glass, or lens, at each end that made distant objects appear larger than they actually were. Galileo was so impressed, he set about making his own version. He decided to demonstrate his invention in Venice. On August 21, 1609, he took a group of nobles to the top of the bell tower of St. Mark's church. Everyone gasped as they looked through the telescope and saw distant buildings and islands looming up before them, impossibly large and very clear. They immediately raised Galileo's salary!

Galileo's spyglass was set in an ivory frame, with two telescopes strapped to a stand.

In debt

Galileo loved romantic Venice, and on one of his many trips to the watery city, he met the beautiful and vivacious Marina Gamba—or "my little, pink **prawn**," as he affectionately called her. Marina liked Galileo so much she came to live with him in Padua. Together they had three children: Virginia, Livia, and Vincenzo. His family responsibilities made his debts worse. On top of that he was expected to provide for his lazy brother's eight children. Eventually Galileo ran out of money and had to sell his daughters to a convent, which broke his heart.

"I bet everyone was impressed with Galileo's inventions," said Digby.

"Not everyone," said Mr. Rummage. "Yes, he was living at a time when people were curious about science. But even so, when Galileo challenged ideas that had been around for a thousand years, he offended many educated people."

"It's a bit like the dinosaurs. Some people still don't believe they really existed, do they?" said Hannah.

"That's because many people find change a bit scary," explained Mr. Rummage.

Science revolution

Galileo lived at a time when scientists and inventors were discovering more and more about the universe. He knew that new discoveries change the way we see and think about things. He tried to persuade people that scientific knowledge must change as new evidence comes along. After all, he, like all scientists that came after him, spent his life testing ideas, changing them and sometimes throwing them away altogether, in his search for the truth.

Aristotle's ideas

For almost 2,000 years, the ideas of the Greek philosopher Aristotle were considered to be the final truth in science. Aristotle believed that Earth was the center of the universe, and that the Sun, the stars, and the planets moved around it in a perfect circle. He also said that the Moon, stars, and planets were perfect and unchanging. The Christian Church liked this idea because it put Earth and the people on it at the center of God's creation.

The Copernican system, which Galileo believed, shows the Sun at the center, circled by the planets.

The Greek system of the universe shows Earth at the center, surrounded by the elements of water, air (clouds), and fire. Around Earth revolve the Moon, Sun, and five planets.

Copernicus's ideas

In 1543, a Polish astronomer called Copernicus made a huge leap forward in the understanding of the universe. He realized that the way the planets moved could only be understood if the Sun were at the center of the universe. Everything else, including Earth and the other planets, moved around the Sun. He also believed that all of the planets in space were continually changing. The problem was that if he was right then the Church was wrong. The Church was frightened of change. They said Copernicus's ideas were wrong, and banned his books.

 # Stargazer

Although Galileo's telescope was probably no better than a cheap amateur's telescope you might buy today, it allowed him to make some amazing discoveries. They were so sensational, in fact, that they shocked the scientific world and upset the leaders of the Catholic Church. Apparently, what Galileo saw so disturbed some church officials, they refused to even look through the telescope. They believed that only the Devil himself was capable of making anything appear in the eyepiece of the telescope, so that it was best not to look through it at all!

Star map showing the constellation of Cancer, the Crab.

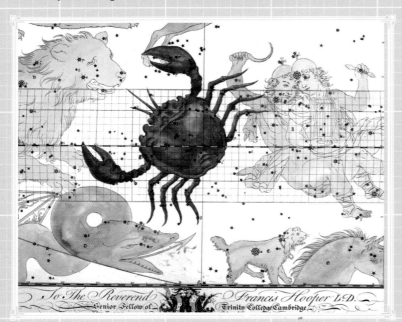

Stars and galaxies

When Galileo focused his telescope on the night sky, he was amazed. He saw, for instance, that the great "cloud" called the Milky Way was made up of countless stars that had never been seen before. From his observations, he realized that the stars were not fixed, as people had thought, but constantly moving. He even mapped the patterns, or **constellations**, some of the stars made in the sky.

Starry Messenger

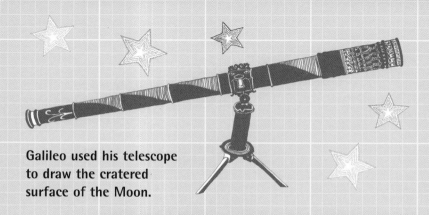

Galileo used his telescope to draw the cratered surface of the Moon.

The discoveries that Galileo made were written down in a small book he called the "Starry Messenger." It was published in Venice in 1610. The booklet caused quite a storm, and it made him famous.

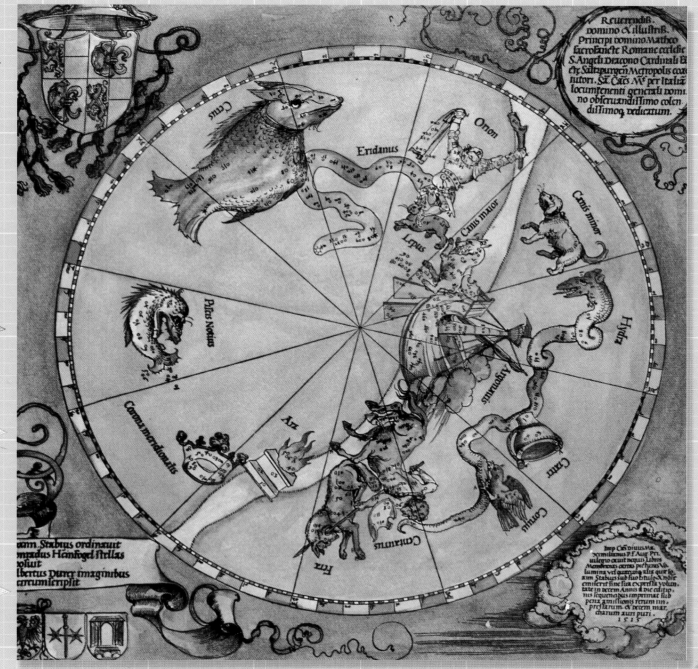

"Galileo really shook things up, then," said Hannah. "I bet all those stuffy church officials were having a fit. It must have been hard to argue against what you could see with your own eyes."

"With the help of a telescope, of course," said Mr. Rummage, "he made massive discoveries, such as the pockmarks he saw on the Moon."

"Zits on the Moon?" laughed Hannah. "Just as well he didn't see Digby's face. He'd have burned his telescope!"

"They're freckles, not pimples!" yelled Digby, indignantly.

"Quite so," interrupted Mr. Rummage. "Anyway, the pockmarks Galileo saw were actually mountains and valleys on the Moon. He also found the Moon wasn't pure and white at all, but lit up by the Sun. And then he noticed that there were dark spots on the Sun that always seemed to be in a different place. This told him the Sun was spinning on its axis.

So it made him think that if the Sun was spinning, then probably Earth was too, just as Copernicus had said."

Galileo's observatory
Spying on Saturn

When Galileo began investigating the planets, he was amazed by what he saw. He observed that Jupiter had four moons. He also saw what seemed to be ears on the planet Saturn. What he did not realize was that he was seeing the bands of gas that surround Saturn—its "rings," as we call them today.

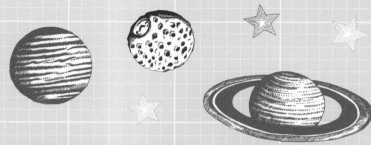

The phases of Venus

When he observed Venus, Galileo found that the planet had **phases** just like our Moon. He saw that sometimes it appeared as a crescent shape, sometimes as a half disc and sometimes fully round, then it changed back to a sliver of light again. This, he noted, depended on the planet's position in relation to the Sun. He worked out that these changes could only mean that Venus was actually revolving around the Sun, making the lit up areas constantly change in size and shape. Galileo said that what he found proved Aristotle's ideas were wrong and Copernicus's theory was correct—the Sun was indeed at the center of the universe.

"But the Sun isn't at the center of the universe," said Hannah, "just our solar system. So he was wrong there."

"Yes, he was," replied Mr. Rummage, "but we know far more about the cosmos today than he did then. Nevertheless, Galileo got closer to the truth of things than any scientist before him—even if he did put a lot of people's noses out of joint."

"There must've been someone who believed in him, though," said Digby. "Not everyone could have been that stupid."

"Oh, yes," said Mr. Rummage, "he had a lot of friends, and many of them in high places. For instance, he was popular with Italy's ruling families, especially the Medicis of Florence. He even called the moons of Jupiter he'd found, the *Medicean stars*. In fact, Galileo was the star attraction at court. Everyone wanted to look through his telescope and hear about his discoveries. His advice was sought on many grand projects and he often tutored the sons of well-to-do families."

"Sounds like he had a good time," said Hannah. "I'd love someone like that to teach me science."

Patrons of science

The powerful Medici family ruled the city of Florence as far back as the 12th century. They had become rich and influential as bankers and businessmen and used their wealth and power to finance, or **patronize**, the development of science and art. Galileo, and most scientists of the day, depended on the generosity of their patrons to earn a living.

Horoscope-reader

The Medicis had their own court **cosmographer**, who studied the stars and planets and their movements. He would read the signs in the sky and would advise the family to make decisions when their stars looked favorable—rather like reading a modern day **horoscope**!

Court mathematician

Galileo's prize pupil was Cosimo de Medici. He was naturally curious and studied hard. Cosimo respected his teacher and made him his court mathematician. Later, Galileo named a comet after Cosimo and dedicated many of his science books to the Medici family.

Ferdinand II

Ferdinand de Medici, Cosimo's son, was inspired by Galileo to set up the Academy of Experiments in 1657. This was the first of the scientific academies that later sprung up around Europe. Ferdinand tried his best to help Galileo when the astronomer got into trouble with the Church. But he was not powerful enough to save Galileo from arrest and imprisonment.

"It must have been hard for Galileo with everyone against him," said Digby. "Why didn't he just move somewhere else?"

"That would have been impossible," said Mr. Rummage. "In those days, Europe was the center of civilization; it wouldn't even have crossed Galileo's mind to go elsewhere. There was no America as we know it because the continent had only just been discovered. No, he had to stay where he was and put up with stubborn churchmen. Although not all of them wanted Galileo thrown to the lions."

"So a few people did stick up for him, then," said Hannah.

"Well, he often had audiences with Pope Urban, who was most interested in the books Galileo wrote and about what was happening in the world of science," explained Mr. Rummage.

"So popes were interested in science as well as religion," said Hannah.

"Popes were interested in most things: science, politics, religion," continued Mr. Rummage. "Pope Urban, for instance, held his own private meetings with mathematicians, astronomers, and other scientists who checked Galileo's work. What went on between him and Galileo behind closed doors was one thing, while what was said officially was another."

"But that's being hypocritical." said Hannah.

"What's that?" asked Digby.

"It's like calling you a smart scientist to your face, when you're just my irritating little brother," giggled Hannah.

"Hey, stop making fun of me!" yelled Digby.

Taking risks

Galileo was careful not to criticize the Church or say that the Bible's description of the world was wrong. He was too smart for that—and in any case, he had a religious upbringing. He thought the Bible was full of different meanings and should be open to interpretation. In those days, making judgements like this was very risky. Non-churchmen were not allowed to interpret scripture, and some people thought that this was what Galileo was doing.

Lucky break

Luckily, though, Pope Urban had given Galileo permission to continue his research—and Galileo was smart enough to make sure he had his permission in writing! Eventually Galileo was cleared of wrongdoing, but he was warned to be careful of what he wrote in the future. The Pope was very interested in Galileo's discoveries, but, in public, he had to show he was against new ideas. Urban told his cardinals to warn Galileo that he must teach the Copernican system as an idea only—not as the scientific truth.

Cardinal's warning

Despite his caution, Galileo's belief in the Copernican system soon got him into deep trouble with the Catholic Church. His views were criticized from the pulpit by preachers, and he was accused of heresy: holding beliefs that are opposed to the beliefs of the Church.

"What's the point of teaching people something and then saying it's only an idea. That's like saying 'I don't actually think I'm right,'" said Hannah. "Why not just tell the truth? I would."

"Then you'd have probably lost your head," said Mr. Rummage.

"Or been burned at the stake," said Digby. "They did that in those days, didn't they Mr. Rummage?"

"They did indeed," agreed Mr. Rummage, "but Galileo had a few tricks up his sleeve. He didn't want to be punished, but he still wanted people to know about his work. So instead of writing a scientific paper, he wrote a book and disguised his ideas as a conversation between make-believe characters."

"Brilliant!" said Hannah. "So it looked just like a kind of story or a play."

"Right," said Mr. Rummage. "Galileo created three characters. The character that told his side of the argument was smart, witty, and brilliant. A second character was able to see both sides of the argument; the third, which argued against Galileo's system, was foolish and bossy, like all of Galileo's enemies—he was called Simplicio."

"What a great name!" cried Hannah.

"Now I know what to call Digby when he's being silly."

"Very funny!" grumbled Digby.

"Hmm," said Mr. Rummage, "I think we'll get back to Galileo's book, if you don't mind. Of course, the Pope banned it because he suspected the foolish Simplicio was based on himself!"

"Bad move, then," said Hannah.

"Yes, Galileo was summoned to stand trial in Rome before the dreaded Inquisition. He made excuses by saying he was ill, and later by saying he couldn't travel to Rome because of the plague."

"Knowing him, I bet he got a note from his doctor," grinned Hannah.

Dangerous book

When Galileo began to write his famous *Dialogue* he was old, poor, and often sick. It took him six years to complete the work. Galileo was careful to send his work to the Pope in Rome for corrections. As soon as the book arrived, the Pope was offended because he said the character of Simplicio, who represented the beliefs of the Church, had a name which meant "fool" in Italian!

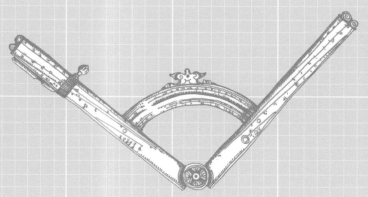

Caught out at last

Over the years, Galileo met Pope Urban six times, and even dedicated a book to him. Urban probably led Galileo to believe that the Church would not interfere with his work, but it did. Perhaps the Pope was more open to new ideas than his priests and bishops, or perhaps he was trying to catch Galileo out—we don't know. Galileo's *Dialogue* was probably the last straw, and, before he knew it, he was summoned to court in Rome.

On trial

Galileo's ideas offended the Church. He was arrested and brought before the Inquisition. The Inquisition was a panel of judges whose job it was to find out whether someone was breaking the laws of the Catholic Church. If Galileo was found to be guilty of heresy, which could include criticizing the Church or writing books about forbidden subjects, he would be severely punished. In those days, many people were tortured and put to death by the Inquisition.

The sentence

At first Galileo defended himself strongly and said scientific discoveries should not be ignored. Weeks of threats and questioning wore him out. When the Inquisition banned him from writing, and ordered all his books to be publicly burned, he felt humiliated. Eventually, Galileo was forced into saying that he might have made his arguments too strongly. He even offered to prove his ideas were wrong—in his next book. Some people think Galileo made this suggestion because he was being clever and looking for a way to keep on writing!

Punishment

The Inquisition forced Galileo to admit all his ideas were wrong in public. But at the end of his confession he was heard to mutter: "And yet it moves," referring to Earth moving around the Sun. His punishment was imprisonment for the rest of his life.

"Those Inquisition people don't sound very nice," said Digby.

"They could be terrifying," agreed Mr. Rummage. "Even though they were monks, their job was to force people to confess to breaking the law; and if they'd already made their minds up, the poor prisoner didn't stand a chance."

"I suppose Galileo was a bit like that," said Hannah.

"He was," said Mr. Rummage. "The Church already called him a heretic—a lawbreaker—for teaching a different view of the world from what was in the Bible."

"What about Pope Urban? Couldn't he help?" asked Digby.

"He could have, I suppose," said Mr. Rummage, "but his job was to promote Roman Catholicism, not to promote science. So, in the end, Galileo had to say he was wrong and the Church was right."

"What!" exclaimed Hannah, "he actually gave in? I don't believe it. Why couldn't he just stick to his guns?"

"He must've been afraid of the Church," said Digby. "After all they probably told him he'd go to hell if he didn't change his mind, or that he'd be burned at the stake."

"Do you think he was a coward, Mr. Rummage?" asked Hannah.

"No, he really had no choice. He couldn't work if he was dead or in prison. And he probably still believed in God. So I don't think he was a coward."

"Me neither," said Hannah.

31

House arrest

Galileo was an old, sick man, and the Church authorities were sympathetic. Instead of clapping him in chains, they put him under house arrest with the Archbishop of Sienna, who kept a friendly eye on him! Eventually Galileo was allowed back to his farm at Arcetri. Shortly after his return home, his beloved sister died. This was a big blow as she had supported him through his many illnesses. Galileo found it difficult to work after the loss, but eventually took up his pen again and began on another book, his *Discourses*.

Reward!

Galileo did not give up easily. It was not long before a Dutch publisher made a secret visit to his home. The Dutchman agreed to smuggle the *Discourses* out of Italy and publish it in Holland. Meanwhile, Galileo's book on machines had become a bestseller in France. Later, when Galileo sent a scientific paper to Holland, the Dutch government sent it back, but awarded him a gold chain worth 500 **florins** for his effort. Galileo accepted their decision—and also the consolation prize!

Freedom refused

Shortly afterward, Galileo sent another paper to Holland and this one was published. He soon received another gold chain from the Dutch government. This time, however, he tactfully refused to accept it—and got the Pope's approval for doing so! Galileo saw his chance to gain back his freedom and begged the Pope to release him. The Pope refused, even though Galileo was now totally blind. Instead, he was allowed to attend church during religious festivals—provided he did not talk to anyone!

"At least he wasn't put behind bars," said Hannah.

"No, but he couldn't leave the house he was living in either. He may have been comfortable, but he had no freedom," explained Mr. Rummage.

"Do you think he had a nice house?" asked Digby.

"I expect so, he didn't just sit around, though," said Rummage, "he began writing his *Discourses.*"

"That took some nerve," said Hannah."

"Well, it was a book on mathematics, which was a safer subject than science. Still, he couldn't push his luck too far as the Archbishop was always looking over his shoulder. Although by that time he was almost totally blind and not much of a threat to anyone," said Mr. Rummage.

"That's so sad," said Hannah.

"And even sadder when you think his blindness was probably the result of him looking at the Sun too often through his telescope," said Mr. Rummage.

"Poor old Galileo," said Hannah looking sorrowfully at the telescope in her hand. "He gave so much to science, yet he died a prisoner in his own house."

"And no one was allowed to believe him," said Digby. "Incredible!"

"Galileo was at the cutting edge of a scientific revolution," said Mr. Rummage, "and generally people don't like changes, especially big ones."

"He could prove he was right, couldn't he?" asked Hannah.

"Yes, but proof isn't always enough," replied Mr. Rummage. "Sometimes you have to change the way people think before they will accept things—even if the evidence is staring them in the face."

"Yeah," said Digby, "like some people are still trying to tell us that no one has actually got to the Moon."

"Well, I'm going to prove lots of things when I'm an astronomer," said Hannah. "And I'll start with this telescope. It's my turn to take something home today, Digby."

"OK, it's yours," smiled Digby. The kids waved goodbye to Mr. Rummage, and as they walked back through the market, Hannah couldn't take her eyes off her new possession.

"You know," she said to her brother, "I like the idea of changing people's view of the world!"

Ahead of his time

Galileo died in 1642, condemned as a heretic. He had made some of the most important discoveries the world had seen, but few people were prepared to give him the benefit of the doubt. In his will, Galileo wrote that he wanted to be buried in the family tomb, next to his father in the church of Santa Croce, but his family feared this might cause problems with the Church—and they were probably right. Instead, his body was hidden, and finally buried nearly 100 years later, in 1737. Some churchmen still were not happy with the idea.

On October 31, 1992, 350 years after Galileo's death, Pope Paul II admitted in a speech that the inquisitors and their advisors had made errors in the case of Galileo.

Galileo's legacy

It was not until 1822 that the Church finally lifted the ban on Galileo's *Dialogues*. By that time, of course, it was common knowledge that Earth moved around the Sun. It was not until 1993 that the Catholic Church formally and in public cleared the astronomer of any wrongdoing. That was three years after the Galileo rocket blasted off on its way to the planet Jupiter.

Galileo did not invent the idea that Earth orbited around the Sun. A Greek astronomer, Aristarchus, had actually proposed the idea 1500 years earlier, and it was Copernicus who said it was the only way to explain the movements of the planets. Galileo made use of his development of the **refracting** telescope to discover new facts about the heavens that would prove the old ideas wrong, and lead to a new understanding of the universe we live in.

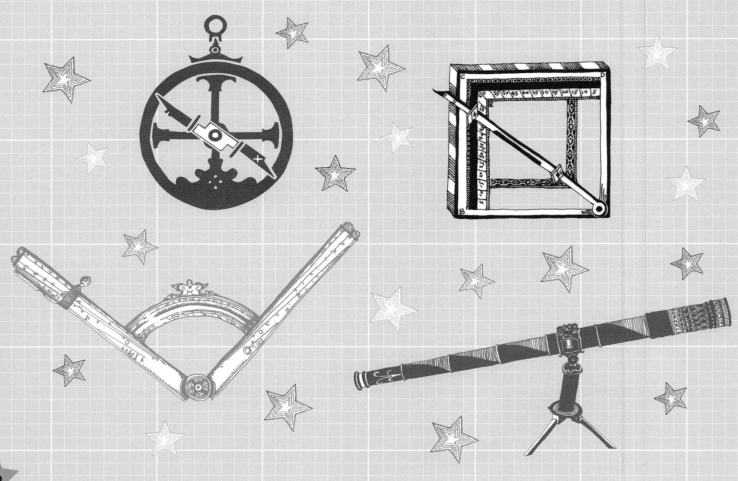

Glossary

astronomer A scientific observer who studies the universe, space, planets, and stars in outer space

constellation A group of stars in the sky that form an easily recognizable pattern

cosmographer A person who makes maps of the universe

crowns Coin currency

dowry Money or property given by a bride to her husband when they are married

florins A type of gold coin

horoscope The prediction of a person's future determined by the position of the stars and planets at the time of their birth

mathematician A person who studies mathematics

patronize To financially support and encourage a scientist, or artist

phase The amount of light that changes the appearance of an object, or planet, in space

physicist A scientific observer who studies the science of matter, energy, motion, and force

prawn A small crustacean animal that looks like a shrimp but with pincers

refracting Bending and changing the direction of a ray of light with a lens

sextant An instrument with a pivotal 60 degree arm used for determining a ship's location by measuring the horizon and an object, or planet, in the sky. Sailors often used the Sun to calculate their location

Index

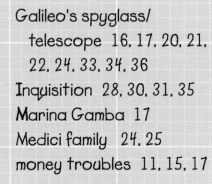

Other characters in the Stories of Great People series.

KENZO the barber has a wig or hairpiece for every occasion, and is always happy to put his scissors to use!

Mrs. BILGE pushes her dustcart around the market, picking up litter. Trouble is, she's always throwing away the objects on Mr. Rummage's stall.

Mr. CLUMPMUGGER has an amazing collection of ancient maps, dusty books, and old newspapers in his rare prints stall.

CHRISSY's vintage clothing stall has all the costumes Digby and Hannah need to act out the characters in *Mr. Rummage*'s stories.

YOUSSEF has traveled to many places around the world. He carries a bag full of souvenirs from his exciting journeys.